Anne M.

A Medley of Rhymes for the Children

Anne M.

A Medley of Rhymes for the Children

ISBN/EAN: 9783337219451

Printed in Europe, USA, Canada, Australia, Japan

Cover: Foto ©Thomas Meinert / pixelio.de

More available books at **www.hansebooks.com**

A Medley of Rhymes·

FOR THE CHILDREN.

WRITTEN AND TRANSLATED BY

A. M.

LONDON :

JAMES NISBET & CO., 21, BERNERS STREET. W.

MDCCCLXX.

LONDON :
KELLY AND CO., PRINTERS,
GATE STREET, LINCOLN'S INN FIELDS. W.C.

TO

MY NIECES AND NEPHEWS,

FROM THEIR LOVING

AUNT ANNE.

1870.

CONTENTS.

A

MEDLEY OF RHYMES.

The Message.

THE blooming flower, with fragrant lip,
　　Whispered some words to me—
The happy bird, with gladsome voice,
　　Warbled them from the tree.

The river, as it onward went
　　Its pleasant, winding way,
Sang with a smile of sweet content
　　That message day by day.

On mountains high, in valleys low,
　The same small voice I heard,
And by the sea, the waves to me
　Spoke out the wondrous word.

I looked upon the silent night,
　And in the heavens above,
In golden letters, clear and bright,
The stars, in lines of shining light,
　Repeated " God is love."

The Seed and the Flower.

Mamma, I've often heard you say
That God is listening when we pray;
And if I do indeed believe,
That what I ask I shall receive.

Why will He not, then, take away
My naughty, sinful heart, to-day;
And make me humble, meek, and mild,
A quiet and obedient child?

I ask Him every day and night
For a new heart, all clean and white;
You know I have not got it yet:
God hears my prayer—can He forget?

2

MOTHER.

No, darling, God does not forget,
Although he has not answered yet;
And if you listen I will try
And tell you now the reason why.

I once pulled up a garden weed,
And in its place I dropped a seed;
Because they told me God's great power
Could change that seed into a flower.

I was a little child, you know,
And thought the seed would quickly grow;
But days and weeks passed slowly round,
And still it lay deep in the ground.

At length there came some gentle rain,
And when the sun shone forth again
I hastened to that spot alone,
Where my little seed was sown.

And there I saw the softened ground
Raised in a gently heaving mound ;
And in the middle there was seen
Two little leaves of brightest green.

And day by day, and hour by hour,
I watched, until there came a flower ;
And thought how good that God must be
Who sent such pretty flowers to me.

And now, my dear, your little prayer
Is like the seed I dropped in there ;
God gives it in your hand to sow,
And promises the seed shall grow.

And as you wait, and watch, and pray,
The seed is springing day by day ;
And God will bless it, like the flower,
Both with the sunshine and the shower.

Then, in the Resurrection bright,
You'll find a heart both pure and white;
And evermore your song will be—
" How very good was God to me ! "

Prayer for a Sick Child.

Lord ! stay the fever wild ;
    Be near us when we weep ;—
    And let some quiet sleep
Fall on our little child.

Thou carest for the bird,
    Rocked safely in its nest,
    It takes its peaceful rest :
Oh ! let my prayer be heard !

The very smallest flower
    Receives, each day, anew
    The cool, refreshing dew
From Thy sustaining power.

Are we not dearer far,
  Father in heaven above,
  Unto thy heart of love,
Than birds and blossoms are?—

O God! I will be still;
  She is not only mine,
  All that I have is thine,
Do Thou thy holy will.

A Child's Remonstrance.

I DO not care to learn the names
　　Of every twinkling star ;
I want to picture in my mind
　　What wondrous worlds they are.
How in the fields of space they hang—
　　How noiselessly they roll—
How they obey that mighty Power
　　Which holds them in control.

And in that sky so darkly blue,
　　I strive those depths to see,
Where stars are waymarks for the mind
　　To pierce infinity.
And though the effort be in vain,
　　While every twinkling light,
But serves to show me with a smile,
　　Some greater deep or height;

Yet not in vain do I come back
  From wandering in the skies,
If from Almighty power I learn
  Almighty love to prize.
For He who guides those countless stars
  Throughout the pathless air,
Takes pleasure in the humblest child
  That rests upon His care.

God is Light.

Said a little child unto me—
  "If God lives so very far
Up above the highest heaven,
  Far beyond the brightest star,

" How can He be always near me,
  Caring for me night and day?
Are you sure that God can hear me
  When I lift my hands and pray?"

And I answered, " God has spoken
  Holy words that we receive;
And He gives us many a token
  To persuade us to believe.

" Like the sun that shines around us,
    Making all things bright and fair,
By the wayside, in the chamber,
    God is with us everywhere.

" Trust Him, darling, when He tells you
    He is near by day and night ;
Distance cannot part you from Him,
    Darkness hides not : ' God is Light !' "

The Skylark.

PART I.

CHILD.

MAMMA ! look at that little bird
That's flying up so high ;
One moment it is on the earth
The next is in the sky.

Its nest lies low among the flowers,
And its little ones are there ;
Why does it leave that pretty home
To wander in the air ?

MOTHER.

My child that bird is taught by God,
Who formed its feathery wings,
To praise His name who gave it life,
So, as it flies, it sings.

And gladly doth it leave its nest,
  And its little ones, I know,
Swiftly to fly, up in the sky,
  Through the mists and clouds below.

And when the purer air it breathes
  It rests upon its wing,
And catches in some little notes
  Of what the angels sing ;

And its voice sounds out more full and free,
  When back to earth it flies,
As it tries to learn the angel notes
  It heard up in the skies.

Some other time I'll tell you how
  Our voices should be heard,
When we strive to reach the purer air
  Just like the little bird.

PART II.

CHILD.

MAMMA, you said you'd tell me how
    To reach the purer air—
I have not wings like the little bird,
    So how can I get there?

MOTHER.

My child, your thoughts are something like
    The little skylark's wings;
And you know they very often fly
    Away to foolish things.

But if you lift them up to Heaven,
    And think of who lives there,
Then that is trying, like the bird,
    To reach the purer air.

And Jesus Christ, who dearly loves
  To hear an infant pray,
Will listen to the simplest word
  That you have got to say ;

And come and whisper in your mind
  About such glorious things,
Far sweeter than the sweetest notes
  The happy angel sings.

But always bear in mind, my love,
  When you read or hear His word,
To try and practise what you learn,
  Just like the little bird.

The Apple Pie.

Now, children dear, come round me here,
    And I will tell to you,
The story of an apple pie ;
And, ah ! dear me, it makes me sigh
    To think the tale is true.

There lived, not very long ago,
    But very far away,
Two children who, like some of you,
Had hardly anything to do
    But jump about and play.

C

One day Aunt Mary was to come,
   They heard with great delight;
And John, and Bessie, were to be
Allowed to stay downstairs to tea,
   And welcome her that night.

Mamma, she thought an apple pie
   For supper would be fit,
But, poor John and Bessie said,
" Alas ! we both shall be in bed,
   And never taste a bit ! "

The pie was made, and put away
   Upon a shelf with care ;
The children by the window stood,
And, oh ! it smelt so very good
   As it was cooling there ;

That Johnny said, " I really think
 I will go in and see
If I can raise the top a bit,
Then we can get a taste of it;
 Come, Bessie, come with me ! "

And so they went, they got a spoon,
 And turn by turn they ate—
It was so good they ate, ah, me !
Until they only left, you see,
 The pie crust and—the plate !

They waited for Aunt Mary long;
 When she at last did come,
She begged Mamma would let them stay
With her to supper, for that day ;
 The children both were dumb.

Poor Johnny's cheeks got burning red,
　　He glanced at every one;
But little Bessie hung her head,
And to herself she quickly said,
　　" Oh ! what will now be done ?"

The pie was brought, and then Papa
　　Began to help it soon;
He cut the crust, and said, " My dear,
What sort of apple pie is here ?
　　I only see—a spoon ! "

The spoon ! ah, me ! the children both
　　Were startled at that sight;
For now they knew the silent Eyes,
That looked upon them from the skies,
　　Had brought their sin to light.

And now I will not tell you more,

    But hope you all will try

To learn the lesson of my song,

And think, when tempted to do wrong,

    About that apple pie !

Minnie to her Dolly.

———◆———

WELL! Alice, my dolly,
    How are you to-day ?
I will come and sit by you,
    And chatter away.
I will just fetch the footstool
    And sit at your feet ;
While you rest on the sofa
    And smile to me, sweet.

Your hair is so pretty,
　　Your eyes are so blue,
Your cheeks are so rosy,
　　Your frock is so new,
You're the prettiest dolly
　　I ever did see;
Who can be so happy,
　　I wonder, as me!

But yet, my dear dolly,
　　You must not be vexed
If I tell you the thought
　　That comes to me next.
Though your hair is so pretty,
　　And your eyes are so blue,
I would rather be Minnie
　　Than I would be you!

You can't see the flowers,
   When they come up in spring;
You can't hear the birdies,
   How sweetly they sing;
Nor run out of doors
   To look in the sky,
And see the white clouds
   As they pass swiftly by.

You have no kind papa
   Or mamma to be near,
To love you, and teach you;
   So, dolly, my dear,
Though your cheeks are so rosy,
   And your dress is so new,
I would rather be Minnie
   Than I would be you !

The Happy Child.

I AM a happy, little child ;
  Who is it makes me so ?
Jesus—who lives above the sky,
Who taught the little birds to fly,
  And made the daisies grow.

The little birds can fly and sing,
  The flowers are sweet and fair,
But yet they cannot learn of God,
  Or thank Him for his care ;
But I can learn about his love,
  And thank Him in my prayer.

Mamma will teach me more and more
  About His love to me;
And I will try through all the day
  Happy and good to be;
For when I am a naughty child
  The God in Heaven can see.

Prayer.

Lord Jesus, look upon me,
  And teach me how to pray;
And may Thy Holy Spirit,
  Drive foolish thoughts away.

My heart is often naughty,
  And filled with passion wild;
O Jesus! do Thou make me
  A holy, happy child.

I am so very helpless,
  Lord, take me as I am;
Be Thou my gentle Shepherd,
  And I Thy little lamb.

And all this day be near me,
To keep me by Thy care ;
Bless every friend that loves me,
And answer this my prayer.

The Boy and the Bird.

THE snow was deep upon the ground,
  The pure, untrodden snow,
When, nestled in his downy couch,
  My child was lying low—
My youngest child,—I did not think
  He was so soon to go.

For blithe and free as any bird,
  How gaily would he sing,
And through the house from early morn
  His happy voice would ring.
Ah, me! I hear within my heart
  Its ceaseless echoing.

But still and patient, there he lay,
  With scarce a touch of pain,
Enjoying, with a quiet smile,
  A robin's fearless strain.
I know that I shall see in dreams
  That quiet smile again.

And so, we watched, from day to day,
  With many an anxious sigh,
When suddenly an angel came
  To bear him through the sky.
" Dear Mother !" then he softly said,
  And meekly closed his eye.

The bird beside him piped and sang,
  With restless wing outspread ;
It chirped and fluttered, till at length
  Its noise was quieted.
And, when we looked within the cage,
  The robin, too, was dead !

I gave him up, my darling child,
  The Saviour heard my prayer,
And by His words of tender love,
  Has made me strong to bear.
" Fear not," He said, " I take him home,
  And you shall see him there."

His little body lieth low,
  The turf is overspread ;
I will not murmur, though my boy
  Be numbered with the dead ;
For Christ hath spoken in my heart,
  And I am comforted.

The Syro-Phenician Woman.

SHE fell down at His feet—" O Lord, I pray
That Thou wouldst come and heal my little child ;
A grievous spirit hath her heart beguiled,
And tempts and tortures her by night and day."
He heard, and strangely turned His face away.
At length, " It is not meet," He slowly said,
" That I should cast away the children's bread
To dogs of heathen nations gone astray."
" Truth, Lord," she made reply, " it is not meet ;
But yet, the dogs eat at the Master's feet
The crumbs that fall."   Oh ! radiant look of grace
That rested now upon the Saviour's face.
" Daughter," He said, " arise ! for this thy word,
Go thou thy way in peace, thy prayer is heard."

The Wood Anemone.

THE poets do not sing of thee,
My favourite wood Anemone.
Many pleasant words I've read
On flowers, which grace the garden bed ;
And prettier ones there are on those
Which fill our meadows and hedgerows,
On wildlings of the wood and stream,
That through the tangled grasses gleam ;
But no one spends a thought on thee,
Thou modest wood Anemone !

Then I will tell, my favourite flower,
How beauteous is thy little dower;
How 'neath the trees thy tiny cup
Each morn doth ope its petals up

D

To drink at dawn the early dew,
And thus thy daily strength renew ;
And how these petals do unfold
A little star of purest gold,
That gleameth through the dewdrops bright,
Rejoicing in the morning light ;
And how thou lovest most the shade,
And, therefore, in the wood or glade,
Thy fragile bell is always seen,
Poised upon its stem of green,
And bending o'er its mossy bed,
Gently inclines its silvery head.

But though the shade thou lovest well,
Yet, when the sun illumes the dell,
To thee it is high festival ;
For then thy petals upward dance,
To meet the sunbeam's earliest glance,
Which downward to thy cup doth stream
With a bright emerald tinted gleam,

Telling thee many a tale of love,
From its burning throne of fire above,
And how it liketh well to come
And in thy heart to find a home ;
The leaflets of thy stem are stirred,
When listening to the honied word,
And a faint light doth softly flow
From star of gold, which gleams below.
But the sunlight may not always stay ;
Reluctantly it steals away,
And thou art left alone to dream,
Of the visit of the sweet sunbeam.

And I have seen thy slender form
In meekness meet a coming storm.
Thou dost not raise thy head on high,
To brave the wind that passeth by ;
But folding close thy leaves around,
And bowing humbly to the ground,
In quietness thou waitest there
Till all again is bright and fair.

And when the rain and wind are gone,
Thou lookest up, my gentle one ;
Thy form is then more fair to see
Than when the sunbeam smiled on thee ;
For on thy leaves, and down thy stem,
Shines many a rainbow coloured gem ;
And in thy cup the star appears,
Like beauty smiling through her tears.

Oh ! I would fain resemble thee,
My flower, my sweet Anemone ;—
My strength each morning to renew
By drinking in the early dew ;
Like thee to watch, with wistful gaze,
To catch the bright sun's earliest rays ;
With heart as full of joy as thine
When the sunbeam round my path doth shine.
And when a storm is threatening near,
And my soul is overwhelmed with fear,
To murmur not, but meekly stay
Until that cloud hath passed away ;

And bless His name who thus hath sent
In love each bitter chastisement;
And bid my faith shine out more clear
Than when prosperity was near.

The Lord's Prayer.

Our Father who art in heaven,
Glory to Thy name be given;
Thou who holdest sea and land
In the hollow of Thine hand;—
Yet makest sinful man Thy care,
And listenest to his feeble prayer;
Glory to Thy name be given,
Our Father who art in heaven.

And let Thy kingdom come, O Lord!

May all receive Thy holy word;

May heathen lands beyond the sea

Hear, and believe, and turn to Thee;

Within our hearts, oh! let it reign,

Cleansing from sin's polluting stain :

May all receive Thy holy word,

Thus, let Thy kingdom come, O Lord!

On earth, oh! may we do Thy will,

As angels it in heaven fulfil ;—

What though afflictions dark enshroud,

There is a light behind the cloud—

A voice that whispers, " God is love ! "

Who sends this trial from above,

And bids you trust Him and be still,

And meekly bear His holy will.

Give us this day our daily bread,
With heavenly food may we be fed;
Grant us from Thine exhaustless store
The bread of Life for evermore :
Then, though we may on earth below,
Keen poverty and hunger know,
We will not murmur if we're fed,
Day by day, with heavenly bread.

And, oh ! forgive our sins, we pray ;
For Jesus' sake, take them away ;—
Every trespass we receive,
May we from our hearts forgive ;
Fill our souls with peace and love
To man below, and God above ;
Oh ! forgive our sins, we pray ;
For Jesus' sake, take them away.

When in temptation's snaring road,

Do Thou deliver us, O God!

Alas! we are too prone to stray

From wisdom's narrow path away;

We follow that which we should shun,

And in the ways of folly run;

When in temptation's snareful road,

Do Thou deliver us, O God!

Now, Lord, receive our humble prayer,

May we Thy loving kindness share;

Adoration, blessing, praise,

We give unto Thy name always;

Thine is the kingdom, Thine the power,

And Thine the glory evermore;

The saints in heaven begin the strain,

And all the earth replies—Amen!

A Christmas Hymn.

THE Lord of Life and glory
  Became a little child;
He left His calm, bright heaven,
  For earth storms bleak and wild;
Exchanged the songs of angels
  For tones of sin and strife;
The bosom of His Father
  For a weary, painful life.

Those eyes, so pure and holy,
    With tears were often dim;
And men who should have welcomed
    Despised—rejected, Him :
Yet for the joy before Him
    He patiently endured,
Till angels high sang " Victory ! "
    Salvation was secured.

O ! Lamb of God ! my Saviour,
    Thy death was life for me ;
O ! grant this day may witness
    My life is hid in Thee.
I bring Thee now my spirit,
    All sinful, and defiled,
Lord ! set Thy seal upon me,
    Make me a heavenly child.

TRANSLATIONS.

Grandmother's Knitting Lesson.

LOWENSTEIN.

SLOWLY, gently, little fingers,
   Now be careful how you hold;
What we learn with pain as children
   Gives us pleasure when we're old.

Grasp the needle not so firmly,
   There's a stitch! now bring it through;
What my Maggie cannot manage,
   Margaret—soon will learn to do.

Not so stiffly, little fingers,
    Put the thread around with care,
Cautiously bring out the needle,
    Now, another loop is there.

Ah ! Mamma will be so happy
    When you lay your garland bright,
Down upon her birthday table,
    With these stockings, smooth and white,

Saying, " Now you know the secret
    Grandmamma and I have had ;
Take me in your arms and kiss me,
    O Mamma, I am so glad."

Grandfather's Darling.

LOWENSTEIN.

BREAD and milk are finished quite,
Kiss me now, my heart's delight!
Always first from bed to spring,
Blithe and gay, you darling thing!
Pinafore and frock so white,
Golden hair so smooth and bright;
Mother's hands, with pride and care,
Braided back that golden hair.

Bring your little book and say
Hymn and verses for to-day;—
Quick and perfect, I declare,
Every little word is there.
Teacher will be glad, I know,
When in school you say it so;
Now run off to school with pleasure—
One more kiss, my little treasure!

The Lapwing and the Nightingale.

GLEIM.

A LAPWING said, " I do declare
That ugly nightingale is there ! "
And thrusting forth his crested head,
Thus to the modest bird he said:
" I hope, poor creature, that you see
You are not company for me."
" That's very possible," said she,
And hopped up higher in the tree ;—
And there she sang so loud and clear,
That people came from far to hear ;
Now low and sweet, now full and high,
She flung abroad her melody ;
And all who listened waited long,
Enchanted with the wondrous song.

Meanwhile the lapwing fluttered by,
And tried in vain to catch their eye.
Alas! not one among them stirred,
Or said, " Look at that handsome bird."
They only stayed for that sweet song,
And when it ceased they all were gone.

So, children dear, the spirit's grace
Is fairer than the fairest face.

The Bee and the Dove.

MICHAELIS.

A BEE was sipping honey,—
  The pretty blossom shook,
The bee it toppled over
  Into a tiny brook.

A dove upon her bower
  A leaf plucked from the tree,
She flew unto the brooklet,
  —And dropped it to the bee.

The bee, with many struggles,
  Got on the leaf afloat,
And safely to the margin
  Came the little sylvan boat.

E

The dove was cooing softly
    Within her bower, one day,
A sportsman came so gaily
    With dog, and gun, that way.

He raised the deadly weapon,
    He pointed at the dove—
The bee came swiftly flying
    Upon the wings of love.

She lighted on his finger,
    She darted down her sting,
And, puff! the shot was scattered;—
    ·Our dove was on the wing!

Then welcome every kindness,
    And pay it back with love;
Each one can help another,
    Like the busy bee and dove.

Mother's Grief.

LOWENSTEIN.

She watched beside her little child,
 With many an anxious sigh ;—
" The night is very long," she said,
 Oh ! would that morn was nigh ! "
" O God ! " she prayed, " in whom I trust,
 Let not my darling die."

She listened to the beating heart,
 The breathing, deep and slow,
She bowed her head and prayed again :—
 " Dear Lord ! in joy or woe,
I turn to Thee, and Thou wilt help
 My time of need, I know."

E 2

And then the little child awoke,
    And said :—" O Mother dear,
You must not weep, for in my sleep
    An angel was so near ;
He kissed my burning cheek, and said :
    ' I bring a blessing here.

" ' I come to give you health once more,
    And take away the pain ;
Thy Mother's cry was heard just now
    Through all the angels' strain ;—
It reached the throne of God, and He
    Has sent her joy again.' "

The Sunbeam.

OFT in the dewy morning,
  A silver voice is heard;
The blossoms of the valley,
  By that sweet sound are stirred.
" Unlock your little treasures,
  Shake off each idle dream;—
I come with light to warm you,
  —I am the bright sunbeam.

" I only ask permission
  To rest a little while,
To kiss your lovely blossoms,
  And cheer you by my smile.
My smile hath wondrous power,
  When buds and blossoms die,
To win their fragrance upward
  Into the clear, blue sky."

The Women of Winsberg.

CHAMISSO.

BEFORE the town of Winsberg
   The noble Conrad lay,
With all his mighty army,
   For many a weary day;
For the beleaguered city,
   Though vanquished, would not yield;
The men cried, " No surrender ! "
   Although their fate was sealed.

But hunger came, and famine,
    And pierced them like a thorn ;
They asked the King for mercy,
    He answered them with scorn :—
" My soldiers ye have slaughtered,
    And by my kingly word,
The man that ventures from the gate
    Shall perish by the sword."

The women then drew near him,
    And answered : " Be it so ;—
Our hands are pure from shedding blood,
    Grant us in peace to go."
The King, when moved to pity,
    His anger turned aside,
And to the fearless women
    He graciously replied :—

" The boon you ask is granted,
   And in this time of dearth,
Quit ye the town to-morrow,
   And bear your treasures forth."
And then unto his nobles,
   " My final will ye know,—
The women with their burdens
   Unhindered are to go."

Then on the morrow morning,
   Before the dawn of day,
Just as the eastern darkness
   Was melting into grey,
A drama was preparing,
   That all the world might see
What woman's power, is in the hour
   Of man's extremity.

Forth from the opened gateway
  There slowly moved along,
Just as the sun was rising,—
  A sorely burdened throng.
Each woman, as her treasure,
  Her husband bravely bore ;
And while they beat their safe retreat,
  The children ran before.

" Stop !" to the crafty women
  Cried many a sentry there ;
But to the moving multitude
  The words were empty air.
They broke through every barrier,
  To stop them was in vain ;
With wayward pace, but steadfast face,
  They march toward the plain.

Meanwhile a wrathful horseman
   Spurred onward to the King :—
" So ho ! my trusty herald,
   What tidings do ye bring ? "
But when he heard the tidings,
   A startled laugh laughed he :—
" Alas ! that by a woman
   Outwitted I should be."

The soldiers chafed around him,
   And longed to draw the sword;
" Not so," said noble Conrad,
   A king must keep his word;
What I have said is sacred
   Alike to friend, or foe;
The women with their burdens
   Unhindered are to go."

And thus from reckless bloodshed,
  His kingly crown was pure,—
And thus unto the nation,
  His kingly word was sure.
For in the happy era
  When Conrad did command,
A monarch's word was sacred
  Throughout our Fatherland.

The Conceited Boy Punished.

HEINSIENS.

FRITZ came from school the first half year,
   As learned as could be,
And wished to show to all around
   His great philosophy.

He hardly spoke, this hopeful son,
   Unto his parents kind ;
For he was eager to display
   The treasures of his mind.

And so at dinner he began :—
   " Papa, you think you see
Two roasted chickens on that dish,
   Now, I will prove them three.

First, this is one, and that is two,
   As plain as plain can be;
I add the one unto the two,
   And two and one make three."

" Just so!" replied the Herr Papa,
   " Blessings be on your pate;
So, I take one, Mamma takes one,—
   The *third* put on your plate!" .

The Doves.

LOWENSTEIN.

LIKE a giant's grave the castle
  Stands, with its deserted halls,
Overthrown are tower and rampart,
  Ruin rests upon its walls.
And the north wind chants a requiem,
  Wandering through the lonely place,
Once the seat of strength and beauty,
  Manly strength, and knightly grace.

In the stronghold, where the vassals
  Mustered in their bright array,
Now the raven, and the screech owl
  Build their nests and bring their prey.
And at night the doleful creatures
  Utter their discordant cry,
Where the tuneful Mininsinger,
  Warbled forth his melody.

But there still remains one token
  Of the mighty power of love,
For amid these ghostly ruins
  Still there broods the gentle dove—
As of old—when in her beauty,
  Toying with her falcon tame,
To caress her doves each morning
  Down the castle maiden came.

Ah ! the stronghold is deserted ;—
   Never more, with silken band
Round its neck, the dove shall flutter,
   To be fondled by her hand.
Yet the village children gladly
   Meet amid the ruins grey,
And the loving doves, descending,
   Come to greet them day by day.

Pecking dainty morsels from them,
   Flitting round with quiet grace,
On their lips so softly pressing,
   As upon the lady's face.
Then away, in rapid circles,
   Round the ancient graves they fly,
Messengers from God to teach us
   Love, and peace, and constancy.

The Invitation.

A. KNAPP.

A SIMPLE German peasant sat and heard
His pastor preach upon an Easter morn ;—
The text was from the Gospel of St. John,
When Christ, the risen Lord, calls from the shore
To His disciples toiling on the sea ;
" Children," He says, " have ye got aught to eat ? "
These words sank deep into the good man's heart.
He sat in silent wonder for a while,
And then he prayed :—" O dearest Jesus Christ !
And didst Thou question thus ! " he sadly said ;
" If Thou wast hungry, and would'st deign to come
And be our guest upon next Sabbath morn,
And rest with us, how welcome would'st Thou be !
I am but poor, I have no costly fare
To set upon my board ; yet still that grace

F

Which led Thee down to earth, will not despise
To take what I can give."

He wandered home, and ever as he went
He prayed this prayer, and all the week he prayed;—
But when the last day came he could not rest,
And " Wife," he said, " take now the best we have
Among the fowls, kill, and prepare it well;
Sweep through the house, and pluck the fairest flowers
To beautify the room.   To-morrow morn
A noble guest is coming to our house;
The children must be clean, and in their best,
That He who comes may be received with joy."

The children sprang around :—" O Father dear !
Who is this worthy man ?"   The Mother spake :—
" Now, Father, tell to me what noble guest
Thou hast invited here."   The Father smiled,
But answered not ; only an inward joy
Shone out upon his face.

On Sabbath morning when the church bells rang,
To the dear house of God they all went forth ;
And ever as he went the Father prayed :—
" O dearest Saviour ! come and visit us ;
Thou once hast hungered, would that I might once
Supply Thy need."

But when at length the congregation leave,
The good House-Mother hastens to her home ;
The fowl is done, the broth is thick and good ;
She draws her table forth, and on it lays
A fair white linen cloth.   The clock strikes twelve,
And then she wonders when the guest will come.

The clock strikes one, and now with anxious mind,
She says, " Dear husband, why does he delay ?
The dinner is prepared, the children stand
So hungry here, and no one seems to come.
What do you call your friend ?   I almost think
He is too proud, and does not care for us."

The Father smiles, and to the children says :—
" Be comforted, for He will soon be here ! "
And then he folds his hands in silent prayer,
And raising up his face to heaven, says :—
" O dearest Lord ! come Thou and be our guest,
And let Thy blessing rest upon us all ! "

Hark ! who knocks at the door ?   The Father goes,
And opening wide, behold ! an aged man,
Weary and worn, with reverend silver locks
Adown his neck.   " God bless you all," he says,
" And for the love of Jesus pity me !
I faint with hunger, and have naught to eat ;
I pray you now supply my utmost need."

" Welcome, thou dearest guest," the father said ;
" We have expected thee,—and yonder see,
Thy chair is waiting ; Thou art not too late :
Come in and rest."   And so, with eager haste
And shining eyes, he led the old man in.

And then unto his wife and children said,
" Behold ! for eight days long I have besought
The Lord that He would come, for well I know
He never will refuse, or turn aside
From those who ask Him in.   And, lo ! in this
Poor weary man who now partakes our cheer,
We have as guest the blessed Saviour here !"

Anger.

If from your lips an angry word
Against another shall be heard,
Though repentance drive in a coach and four,
You will overtake it never more.

The Thunderstorm.

SCHWAB.

GREAT grandmother, grandmother, mother, and son,
Met together when day was done;—
The child is busy with innocent play,
The mother looks over her Sunday array;
Grandmother prepares the evening meal,
And then sits down to her spinning wheel;
Great grandmother nods in the old arm chair.
How close is the room! how sultry the air!

The boy, with a shout, says, " Ah ! it is well,
To-morrow will be the Festival !
Then I shall dance, I shall sing, I shall run,
Out in the meadows till daylight is done;
I·shall gather such posies of sweetness and bloom,
And they will look gay in our dull, little room;
My mother will kiss me, and I shall be proud.—
Hark ! do you hear the thunder so loud ?"

The Mother she answers, " Yes ; it is well,
To-morrow will be the Festival !
How pleasant these days of holiday rest ;
I must look out my grandeur, and put on my best :
Many old friends are sure to be there,
Life has its pleasure as well as its care ;
The sky has its sunshine, and sometimes its cloud ;
Hark ! do you hear the thunder so loud ? "

The Grandmother murmured, " I know right well
To-morrow will be the Festival !
My feast days are over, and life to me
Is sorrow, and care, and perplexity ;
I take up my burden, and strive for the best—
Day is for labour, night is for rest ;
I spin for the clothing, and cook for the meal.
Hark ! do you hear that thunder peal ? "

Great Grandmother spake, " I hear them tell
To-morrow will be the Festival ;
Oh ! might I die on that blessed morn,
I am so weary and forlorn ;

The pleasures of life are past and gone,
My work is ended, my day is done."
Look! do you see that lightning flame?
None of them saw it, so swiftly it came;

Its burning kiss is on every face,
Four lives are clasped in that strange embrace;
   The chamber is bright
   With marvellous light,
In the chariot of fire is room for them all,—
They hasten away at the Master's call,
And to-morrow will be the Festival!

LONDON:
KELLY AND CO., GATE STREET, LINCOLN'S INN FIELDS. W.C.

www.ingramcontent.com/pod-product-compliance
Lightning Source LLC
Chambersburg PA
CBHW020253290326
41930CB00039B/1046